The Furnace And Glass In Alchemy

J. W. Hamilton-Jones

Kessinger Publishing's Rare Reprints

Thousands of Scarce and Hard-to-Find Books on These and other Subjects!

- Americana
- Ancient Mysteries
- Animals
- Anthropology
- Architecture
- Arts
- Astrology
- Bibliographies
- Biographies & Memoirs
- Body, Mind & Spirit
- Business & Investing
- Children & Young Adult
- Collectibles
- Comparative Religions
- Crafts & Hobbies
- Earth Sciences
- Education
- Ephemera
- Fiction
- Folklore
- Geography
- Health & Diet
- History
- Hobbies & Leisure
- Humor
- Illustrated Books
- Language & Culture
- Law
- Life Sciences

- Literature
- Medicine & Pharmacy
- Metaphysical
- Music
- Mystery & Crime
- Mythology
- Natural History
- Outdoor & Nature
- Philosophy
- Poetry
- Political Science
- Science
- Psychiatry & Psychology
- Reference
- Religion & Spiritualism
- Rhetoric
- Sacred Books
- Science Fiction
- Science & Technology
- Self-Help
- Social Sciences
- Symbolism
- Theatre & Drama
- Theology
- Travel & Explorations
- War & Military
- Women
- Yoga
- *Plus Much More!*

We kindly invite you to view our catalog list at:
http://www.kessinger.net

PART VI

OF THE FURNACE
AND GLASS

H. VON BATSDORFF

A single small furnace, wherein the degrees of heat can be maintained, is sufficient. Let it be safely placed where no accident can happen from fire. Place an iron pot in your furnace containing sand or ashes, and put your small glass phial therein, and do not take it out until you see the whole mass converted into a beautiful blood-red colour—the sign of ultimate perfection.

PANDORA

During the solution the fire must be gentle, but in the sublimation it must be a little increased, and towards Redness it must be strong.

RADIX CHYMLÆ

During the solution the fire must be soft, in the sublimation middling, in the coagulation temperate, in the White-making steady, in the Rubifying strong. If you are ignorant of the heat you will fail.

LAURENTIUS VENTURA

The heat must be linear unto the end of the work. When the fire is equally kept, the subject, by the action of heat, is the better altered from one nature to another, and that which was humid first will become dry, the black will become white, and the white citrine and red.

WATER STONE OF THE WISE

Place it (the glass) in a convenient furnace and begin with a gentle, continual, airy and vaporous heat; such as a hen causes sitting on her eggs.

95

ESSAY ON ALCHEMY

PANDORA

Begin with a soft heat, until peace is made between the water and the fire [until the principles are united in perfect blackness].

WALCHIUS

A slow heat preserves the natural or radical humidity. The Philosophers require a fiercer heat, such a one as the hen gives to her eggs.

LAURENTIUS VENTURA

As there are many degrees of heat, the question is how it must be—Strong or Gentle? To this we answer that in the beginning the fire must be gentle as **Lullium** says: Know then that without heat nothing is generated. Intense heat causes destruction, and cold is as bad; but temperate heat is pleasant to the body. By a gentle heat the corrupting humidity is extracted. . . . It suffices to administer a continual slow heat, according to the operation of our work—that is a natural heat.

PANDORA

When thou seest the fixt water [the secret Fire] without any ascending thereof fret not about the fire; only have patience until the spirit and the body are become one.

WATER STONE OF THE WISE

Our Aqua mercurii is excited by the help of common external heat, administered by art.

ESSAY ON ALCHEMY

INCERTUS

If you wish to see the sign of putrefaction it is necessary that you procure an external moving heat, for as Nature in the mines boileth by means of a gentle heat, in like manner our philosophical matter receives power to alter itself, from such a degree of artificial heat as may be able to stir up its inward power. This artificial heat must not be violent, but soft and gentle, only able to act on the most subtil particles, to raise and mix them, until the whole composition be broken, divided without any manual separation, and converted into perfect blackness.

PONTANUS

Put it on the fire, [i.e. in the furnace] with such a proportion of heat as shall only excite or stir up the matter, and in a short time that fire [the secret sophic Fire] will complete the whole work.

RADIX CHYMLÆ

The putrefaction of the body is the beginning of the work, and is effected by a gentle heat, so that nothing may ascend in the horse dung, i.e. in our mercury.

[The solution effected by the secret internal fire he here calls horse dung; but the *gentle heat* mentioned is that which is applied externally.]

JOHAN DE MONTE SNYDER

You must be particularly careful about the government of the fire, which must constantly remain in its right degree and must never cease; for if the natural heat should fail, your work will die, and an immature birth will follow, and that which is immature can only work according to its own nature.

INCERTUS MACROCOSMUS

Concerning the fire, I must tell you candidly that *two kinds* of fires are required, an external fire and an internal. The one without the other can effect nothing. The external elemental fire must excite the internal so as to cause it to act, and the external heat must not overpower the internal, as **Count Bernard** says rightly "it must be a steady digesting fire not too vehement."

ALPHIDIUS

Putrefaction is effected in a very low heat, like that of warm and moist horse dung, and in no other, *so that nothing* may ascend.

PANDORA

Put a lamp under your glass; and light it. Keep it burning night and day continually. Take care that it be never suffered to go out.

INCERTUS MACROCOSMUS

When you have put the genuine matter in its proper vessel it then requires only a *natural heat*, so arranged that the external heat may not surpass the internal but only excite it to action. If the heat is too great no alteration can possibly take place. A great heat can only destroy and burn the matter so that nothing useful can come out of it. On the other hand if your heat is too small the materials will be dried up and become hard. The metallic spirits will be dormant and inactive, and cannot operate if not excited [by an external heat] and vivified by a living [internal] fire. As this is of great importance the Artist must be careful not to commit an error in this point, otherwise he will do nothing.

WATER STONE OF THE WISE

Put a small fire under it [the glass] to excite the internal heat, as **Pontanus** says, as a child must be in a natural animal heat in the Mother's womb.

Take care, through the whole work, that you do not increase your heat too much, especially during putrefaction; because, during putrefaction, the internal natural power begins to subtilize the body. Therefore to preserve the internal heat of the bodies from injury be careful, especially during putrefaction to keep a gentle heat.

JOHANNES DE PADUA

Be careful not to make your fire too strong. This would cause the Matter to sublime and would destroy the work. Notice what I say: if you make your fire gentle and govern it prudently that it may not exceed the internal heat [of the secret Fire] you will be certain to bring your work to perfection.

Observe then! as soon as the *internal heat* of your matter or of the body by feeling the power of the external heat awakeneth and begins to act, *the matter has then heat enough to operate perfectly*, conformably to her own nature, and without doubt, to produce its fruit by the power of Nature within. Even if you have made the work ten times before, be not too bold with your heat, but govern it with care, or your work will be destroyed.

H. VON BATSDORFF

The natural or external heat must cause the internal to awaken and to operate. The external heat must not, by too much violence, surpass the internal, or all your labour will be in vain.

EYRÆNEUS PHILALETHA

As the Stone is compared to man, and its first humid regimen to a bath, therefore make the first degree of heat *pleasant, gentle, like a hot bath for a naked person*—which is a lower degree of heat than he can bear, and causes but a gentle sweat.

The second degree is a little higher, whereby a copious perspiration would be induced, and this is as hot as a man can bear it.

The third degree is so much hotter as to cause a hissing and a bubbling and cannot be borne long by the hand; for our composed work in this degree of heat rises in bubbles, which fall down again, rising and falling continually.

The fourth and last degree, which brings dryness, cannot be borne by the fingers without burning them.

[In these degrees this author is here more candid than where he directs (in "**Ripley** Revived") to use such a degree of heat as would keep "tin or lead molten".]

THE SAME

I swear unto thee, upon the faith of an honest man, that if thou urge thy fire so as to make ought sublime, in the days of this regimen [that of Saturn] thou wilt destroy the work irrecoverably; be content then, with good **Trevisan**, to be detained in prison 40 days and nights, and suffer the tender nature to remain below in the bottom [avoiding any kind of sublimation].

LAURENTIUS VENTURA

Our Stone has got its own fire, which, however, is inactive unless excited and moved by external heat.

SENDIVOGIUS

Our blessed work must be conducted agreeably to the four seasons of the year.

The first with us is winter—Cold and humid.

The second, spring, is warm and humid.

The third is the warm and dry summer.

The fourth, Autumn, is the harvest or time for reaping our fruit.

The heat of the first regimen must be like that of a hen sitting over eggs to hatch chickens; or similar to the heat in our stomachs which digests our food. This heat continues until blackness—it may even be continued till the matter is changed into Whiteness; but if this heat be transgressed and the matter be kept too hot, you will never obtain the wished for Raven's head, but either a sudden transient redness, or a red oily matter swimming on the superficies. Perhaps the matter may begin to sublime: in that case the composition may be taken out of the glass and imbibed de novo with our virgin's milk [secret Fire] and then you may recommence the concoction with more prudence, endeavouring to avoid similar errors in future.

When the White appears, you may increase your heat a little, to the second degree, until the matter be perfectly dried up—which heat may be compared to that of the Sun when he goes from Taurus into Gemini. [The degree of heat now spoken of is merely comparative. If his winter heat is equal to that of a hen's on eggs when hatching them, his spring heat must have a proportional increase of temperature. This remark applies equally to what follows]: When the Stone is perfectly dry the fire must be increased again, answerable to the increase of the sun's heat when he passes into Leo.

JOHANNES DE PADUA

In the beginning of the work the first degree of heat must not be higher than the warmth of a sitting hen. In the middle of your stove you must make a door which you can open and shut, so that you can feel in the pot how quick or how gentle your heat is. Let it be such that when you touch the pot your hand may feel pleasantly warm. Attend to what I say or you will greatly damage the work. Take care, above all things, not quickly and rashly to increase your heat; for if you make your fire too intense and the external heat should quickly overpower and conquer the internal heat of the materials, the body would retain the spirit; or else the spirit will sublime, and especially in the end, when the body is converted into a Spirit: therefore be attentive in governing the fire rightly, or you will destroy your work.

ISAACUS HOLLANDUS

There are three colours . . . the first two must be produced by a very low heat, which heat must be increased very gently.

EYRÆNEUS PHILALETHA

See that thy furnace be trusty, else thou mayest and wilt fail; for tho' the fire of coals do not effect anything, yet *it excites*, and the *water* [the mercurial water or secret Fire] though it be of a wonderful nature, yet it acts no farther than as it is stirred up [by the external Fire], and any intermission in this work, after it is begun, will destroy it. Therefore the wise men have called the furnace an *Athanor*, that is Immortal, shewing that from the beginning to the end the fire must not go out.

RIPLEY

Take heed to defend your glass from a violent heat, and a sudden cold: make use of a moderate fire and beware of vitrification.

METALLURGIA

Having prepared your principles, put them, most intimately mixed into a proper glass, so that only one third part of the glass may be filled. Shut the glass closely that nothing may evaporate. Place it in ashes, or in sand, and administer the first degree of heat—such a heat, that, without burning your hand, you may be able to suffer it to rest on the ashes or sand, or on the upper part of the neck of the glass. Keep it in this heat, without moving or disturbing it, until complete blackness and various colours appear, and whiteness follows. It is of great moment that you do not hurry your work and burn up the matter by too much heat. . . . Be careful of your fire that it be not too strong . . . you ought to have blackness with such a heat that you can hardly bear your fingers on the glass, and yet can bear the heat without burning them. This regimen must be continued till you have gone through perfect blackness into dryness, and until the matter is become snow or silver white and fixed, and the Queen is born. This is obtained by one and the same linear heat. Then you must increase your heat, but not out of reason till the matter becomes yellow; and so continue and it will become of the most perfect deep cinnabar or carmine redness, or like unto a quiet glowing fire.

MARROW OF ALCHEMY

. . . beware impatience do not cause
Thee through an itch of mind for to be bold,
In this thy work to transgress Natures laws
For no man sooner errs through heat or cold
   Than he who through impatience of mind
   Cannot expect its time which he would find
Move not thy glass, nor open, else thou wilt
Endamage, may destroy, thy work: beside
Encrease not fire rashly, lest that spilt
Thy work thou see. There's nothing all the Tide
   That this thy work doth stand so much in fear
   As too much fire: one hour will cost thee dear
Beware thy Spirits find not where t'exhale,

For that thy work would spill, and also cause
Much hurt unto the workman. If you fail
Therein, you break one of the strictest laws
    Of all this work: nor cause them so to rise
    As for to break the Glass, which brittle is
Therefore as strong thy glass be sure thou get
As may be, without either knots or flaws,
Equally blown for strength, which thou shalt set
Within a ring of brass, where thou shalt cause
    It to be fixt, with moistened bone-ash: this
    Closely prest down a certain safe-guard is
    . . . With gentle fire thy work assay,
For that is certain. Be not moved with haste
Thy work t'anticipate; no not a day;
But bide with patience till the black be past,
    Then mays't augment thy fire, but not too much—
    Rather too little than too great, for such
The counsel is of all the Sages old.

ARTEPHIUS

You need only to prepare the matter. Nature herself
alone will perfect it: and if she be not hindered by
some contrary thing, she will not overstep her own
proper motion, neither in conceiving, nor in generating,
nor in bringing forth. Therefore, after the preparation
of the matter beware only, lest by too much heat, you
inflame the bath or make it too hot. Secondly, take
heed, lest the spirit should exhale, lest it hurt the
Operator—to wit lest it destroy the work, and induce
many infirmities—as sadness, trouble, vexation, and
discontent. . . . Decoct the composition till it be
invested with a most perfect red colour.

ESSAY ON ALCHEMY

BACON

The vessel for our Stone is but one, in which the whole magistery or Elixer is performed and perfected. . . . Though the philosophers often repeat that the matter is to be put into the vessel, and closed up fast, yet it is sufficient for the operator, *once* to put the said matter in, *once* to close it up and so to keep it, even to the very perfection and finishing of the work. If these things are often repeated the work will be spoiled. . . . Thy vessel being well and perfectly closed, is never so much as once to be opened till the perfection or end of the work. So that you see the vessel is to be kept close that the spirit may not get out.

LAURENTIUS VENTURA

Secure thy vessel that the composition may not escape and fume away, and you will obtain your end.

PANDORA

Mind that your door be well shut that he that is within, may not find his way out, and, if it please God, you will find everything terminate well.

EYRÆNEUS PHILALETHA

It is put into the glass and sealed up before you can attain the first degree of the Magistery.

ANONYMOUS

Put the mercurial matter into a proper glass, seal it and place it in its warm bed for a philosophical month until it begins of itself to ferment and putrefy.

ESSAY ON ALCHEMY
EYRÆNEUS PHILALETHA

Be careful of the closure of the vessel, lest the spirits should fly out and the work be destroyed. Keep therefore the vessel and its ligature, nor look upon this to be of little moment. . . . Consider with how great care Nature has shut the womb of a pregnant woman . . . with no less industry be thou cautious in perfecting this Philosophical work, lest thy labour be in vain.

This is the end of this publication.

Any remaining blank pages are for our book binding requirements and are blank on purpose.

To search thousands of interesting publications like this one, please remember to visit our website at:

http://www.kessinger.net